The Hidden Flower Journal

Discovering the Voice
of the Divine Feminine

This Journal Belongs To

_____

Dedication

For my Heavenly Mother,
you are the Queen of my heart.

For my three earthly mothers,
thank you for teaching me how to be a mother,
and the value of hearth and home.
I miss you every day.

For my husband,
who supports me in every way so that I am able to
embrace motherhood wholeheartedly.
You are giving me a rare and priceless gift.
There are no words to express my gratitude.

For my children,
those of my womb and those of my heart,
thank you for making me a mother.
You are all my dreams fulfilled.

For my grandchildren, those who are in this world,
and those who are yet to arrive -
You are my joy and hope for the future.

The Spirit that never dies
is called the mysterious feminine.
Although she becomes the whole universe,
her immaculate purity is never lost.
Although she assumes countless forms,
her true identity remains intact.
The gateway to the mysterious female
is called the root of creation.
Listen to her voice,
hear it echo through creation.
Without fail, she reveals her presence.
Without fail, she brings us to our own perfection.
Although it is invisible, it endures;
it will never end.
Lao Tzu, Tao Te Ching, Verse 6 [1]

Contents

Preface

In all the world's spiritual traditions, there is a Divine Feminine energy. She is known by many names and has many faces, but her sacred energy dwells in each one of us, whether we believe it to be true or not. In some traditions, she is born human; in others, she is formless and infinite and represents the womb of creation as The Nourisher, the Giver of Life. She has many names from every spiritual path and culture and is often referred to as the Universal Mother, The Mother of Liberation, the Goddess of the Universe, The Queen of Heaven, and The Bride of God, to name a few. She is believed to be full of unconditional love, power, heart centered wisdom, creativity, inspiration, and nurturing energy. The divine genius of the Mother sends angels, defeats negative entities, transforms the illusion of division into oneness, rights all wrongs, heals every infirmity, brings abundance and peace, and protects and defends anyone who calls on her.

The Divine Feminine knows each of her children intimately and wants to exhort us by bringing wisdom, grace, and consolation through intuitive guidance. Our Mother is the voice of encouragement and possibility. She is your closest friend, most trusted ally, your voice of reason, and the wholeness within you. Entering a conscious relationship with her allows you to enter a time of receptivity and transformation - waiting, listening, feeling, and intuiting. She is the loving heartbeat of the Universe. She is the interconnectedness of all. Honoring the Divine Feminine is to honor the ebb and flow of life, to align with the cycles of the moon, to embrace the changing seasons, to shine with the stars in the celestial heavens, to awaken to the most radiant dawn after the darkest night, and to experience your life being transformed from agony to ecstasy.

Allow this contemplative journal be the sacred sanctuary where you feel safe to be vulnerable, delve deep, and be brutally honest with yourself. Let this journal be the sacred space where you record your secret thoughts, highest truths, and the hidden meaning behind everything. May you honor your inner seeker, express your deepest desires, make your most courageous decisions, ponder the purpose of your life and relationships, and explore your soul's wisdom, as you meet your most authentic self. This journal may cause you to reconsider your beliefs, reexamine your world view, and help you to gain the necessary courage to begin to be an observer of yourself and your inner world, where your light and shadow selves converge. You will discover your innate ability to tap into the energy of the Divine Feminine to transmute every form of negativity, heal and release painful memories, and reevaluate your perception of everything. The concepts in this journal will encourage you to step outside of judgement, comparison, and competition to contemplate the soul reason for absolutely everything you have ever done or hope to do. You will begin to embrace a new sense of freedom as you ask big questions and make self-honoring choices that you never knew you could.

The Divine Feminine is The Hidden Flower within each of us. Whether you identify as being masculine or feminine, journaling is a way to care for the sacred garden of the soul, to awaken The Hidden Flower within. Are you ready to become a gentle gardener, ready to tend to your own soul, your highest self, as you discover your own path and purpose? May you embrace this opportunity to open a divine conversation between yourself, the Divine Feminine, your angels, guides, and your entire spiritual team. May this journal be a mirror to your soul, reflecting to you the areas of your life in need of loving care and healing, new awareness of your talents and long forgotten dreams, as well as the guidance needed to pursue your soul mission for this lifetime.

Celebrate yourself and your journey, for your life is truly sacred.

The Vision

It is with great love that I give you this message to share with those who are being called to be my witnesses of love and light. Many are called, but few are chosen to be my instruments of love and healing in this world. It is through, The Hidden Flower Journal, that I will impart my messages bringing hope and joy to all who choose to receive my words of loving guidance.

I love you unconditionally and I bless you with special graces to strengthen you on your sacred journey, and I am with you always. You are my beloved, my child. There is nothing you could ever do to separate yourself from my love. Let us learn together all the ways of love so that you may live your life with purpose and fervor. Allow me to teach you, my child, what It means to love yourself and others without condition. I will bless your soul to be filled with heavenly light so that you may shine on earth brightly and beautifully. Your eyes are the windows through which the love and light of Spirit will shine upon all who come into your gaze. Your heart and eyes will light up the night upon the earth, dissipating the darkness, allowing love to radiate across the earth.

I see souls as lights in this world - some are not as bright as they could be. Allow my love to heal your wounds and to awaken you once again to the power and beauty of your own sacred light within. You must choose to love yourself and others, so that your light may shine brightly. Have you forgotten what it means to love? I will lift the veil of illusion from the world, the veil of fear, so that every soul will awaken to the truth that love is all there is. All else is simply an illusion rooted in various forms of fear. Come, place yourself within My Heart of pure, unconditional love where I will welcome you and heal you and teach you the ways of love.

I am overjoyed to see each soul brighten upon the earth. You are all lights shining in this world. The more you choose to be compassionate, forgiving, and loving, the brighter your light will shine. Your healing and awakening will benefit the entire world, my child. As you become brighter, so too do the other souls in your sphere of influence. You are one with the Creator and you are one with all. Separation and division are rooted in fear. Choose unity and oneness, always. Choose love. Choose to shine your brightest light by learning the ways of love."

Journaling Meditation

The Hidden Flower Journal is a contemplative journal designed to help you to get in touch with your own higher guidance, as well as the wisdom of the Divine Feminine aspect of Spirit. Ask the angels to bless and assist you as you set the intention to be healed, awakened, and placed on the path that will ultimately help you discover your divine purpose. The Divine Feminine, your Mother, will speak directly to your personal spirit bringing illumination and practical guidance for your spiritual growth and expansion, no matter where you are on your sacred journey. Contained within the following pages are fifty-five messages, all of which have something to say to you personally. You may wish to read and work with one each day, or one each week, depending on what comes through the message for you. You may receive hits of intuitive guidance immediately or at night when you are in a dream state because it is easier for some souls to process the messages while their egos are resting. As you take time to internalize the Mother's messages while learning Her ways of love, your self-awareness will expand, and you will receive healing in unexpected, beautiful ways.

Once you have read and journaled about all your insights and concerns, take several deep breaths, while consciously intending to release all stress, tension, indecisiveness, worry, confusion, doubt, and fear - all lower vibrational emotions - to the Divine Feminine, your Holy Mother. It is also helpful to verbally express what you are releasing. When you begin to calm down, say three times: **"I call upon you, Holy Mother, because I know you love me unconditionally. I ask You to help me to calm my mind and center myself as I settle into my heart's wisdom."** Take several deep breaths while consciously breathing in new light to illuminate the situation, while breathing out all of the negative emotions you feel. Now, choose only one problem or issue to focus on. Really narrow your focus on that one thing. Say three times, while also focusing on your breath, **"Holy Mother, I welcome and receive Your nurturing love, grace, and peace now. I welcome and receive new insight, fresh perspective, and guidance that will show me what I need to know now."** Continue breathing and consciously releasing all negative emotions and out of control thoughts. Over a period of several minutes, try to calm and empty your mind so that there is room for new guidance to come in. Feel your soul and the love and wisdom that resides in your heart. Try and connect that energy with your mental energy now. Observe your mind and heart coming together. All that you need is right there.

You Have a Special Light That Cannot be Hidden

MESSAGE 1

"It is time to accept that you have a special calling. You have a special light that cannot be hidden. You must follow your sacred knowing; you already know much more than you realize. Awaken to the beauty and power within, by tapping into your soul's worth and value."

Not all people are aware of their own light. Sometimes we see the light (or lack of it) in others. Some people consciously choose to shine their light, blessing all who come into their presence. Some people purposefully dim their own light, hiding and shrinking, to not be noticed by others. What higher purpose does it serve to remain dim? A certain powerlessness comes over us when other people try to overshadow us, making us feel unworthy. Perhaps they feel threatened by our luminous qualities. Maybe you felt like the black sheep of the family when really you simply have your own unique way of relating to the world and those around you. Perhaps you are still trying to discover how to express yourself in your own creative way. The truth is that our planet needs your unique, radiant essence more than ever. Our job as lightworkers is to shine our light and help other people do the same. What does this mean exactly? It means that every one of us has unique gifts and talents to share, and when you choose to discover them and put them to good use, it benefits everyone around you, and the consciousness of the entire Universe elevates. You are needed, and your light cannot be hidden - it wants to shine more than ever.

Affirmation:

I have a special calling and a special light that cannot be hidden. My gifts and talents are unique. I have so much to give and to share. From this day forward, I choose to shine brightly so that the whole Universe may benefit.

_____

_____

_____

_____

_____

_____

_____

_____

_____

_____

_____

_____

_____

_____

_____

Know Your True Power

MESSAGE 2

"I have been calling you always. You are my light that will be a beacon in this world. You will uncover the secret of knowing your true power. As you discover your own inner truth and reality, which is pure love and light, you will lead others and be an example for all the world to see."

Before we incarnated into our physical body, our soul chose sacred contracts with the Divine based on what lessons our soul desired to learn this lifetime. We are created in the image and likeness of the Divine Masculine and the Divine Feminine, which is the very essence of who we are. It is an illusion to think that we could ever be separated from the love and light of Spirit, and it is natural to hear the voice of the Divine within ourselves. All has been lovingly orchestrated by the intelligence of Spirit to best assist you with your soul journey and mission. How do you find out what you came here to be and do? Is what you are doing now giving you a sense of inner peace? Your purpose may be a paid job, or a hobby or a volunteer opportunity. Your calling may be lived out in a very public way, influencing others on the world stage, or in a quiet way offering support and love from your home by caring for your children or aging parents. All that matters is the love, the kindness, and the compassion that you are sharing with others. The process of remembering your soul purpose is introspective in nature, as the answer lies within you, not without. When you embark on a spiritual journey of self-discovery and soul awareness, you will begin to seek higher guidance and live your life from a place of love. This always leads you toward your true purpose.

Affirmation:

I am grateful for my innate ability to hear higher guidance for myself. I am comforted to know that as I embrace who I am, and make my innate gifts and talents a priority, I will become an example of living my life with passion and purpose.

_____

_____

_____

_____

_____

_____

_____

_____

_____

_____

_____

_____

I Have Called You with a Holy Calling

MESSAGE 3

"You may doubt, at times, that what you are receiving is from me, but know that I have gifted you, and called you with a holy calling. From the time you were born, you have known that you would accomplish something wonderful."

Do you yearn for fame and fortune or the simplicity of being loved by your family and close friends? Do you value having status and making a name for yourself in the world, or do you simply enjoy doing secret, random acts of kindness? For some, just knowing that you have brightened someone's day is acknowledgment enough. I have often heard professional women comment that their new baby is by far their greatest accomplishment. Some people shine their light by traveling all over the world, saving the animals, or advocating for the environment. Perhaps you are shining your light on the corporate culture while building a global empire. You could be one of many doctors, firefighters, police officers or military personnel in a life-saving career, bringing healing or providing safety to those in need of your service. Maybe you are in the entertainment industry, bringing joy to the masses. Perhaps you are a parent, teacher or daycare worker dedicating your life to the formation of youth. You may enjoy working as a counsellor or pastor helping souls to have more self-awareness or a deeper relationship with Spirit. You may own a business or work as a tradesperson using your skills to provide necessities in your community. Perhaps you are a chef, waiter, housekeeper, or bartender in the service industry always offering a smile or a helping hand. Whatever your calling is, at the end of each day, ask yourself, "Did I show love, kindness, and compassion today? Did I make a positive difference?" Do small things with immense love, and your spiritual success is assured.

Affirmation:

I am grateful for my innate ability to hear higher guidance for myself. I am comforted to know that as I embrace who I am and make my inborn gifts and talents a priority, I will become an example of living my life with passion and purpose.

_____

_____

_____

_____

_____

_____

_____

_____

_____

_____

Love and be loved. This is your true purpose.

Every Journey is Sacred

MESSAGE 4

"You will realize that there are those who will never understand you. Their journey is not your journey. Every journey is sacred. Your journey this life is to accomplish certain things necessary to bring light and grace to the people I bring to you."

If you are on an accelerated spiritual path this lifetime, you are likely no stranger to suffering and adversity. Perhaps you have changed locations many times (which helps you learn spiritual lessons more quickly) and experienced grief too many times to count. If your soul has suffered one or more dark nights of the soul then you are likely stronger, and more compassionate, and less judgmental, as well. Some people stay in the same place with the same partner for their entire life. Some are very career-oriented, while others value family above all else. Do you know of at least one person that seems to coast through life with no obvious responsibilities? What about the people that have never lost anyone or experienced illness other than a common cold? All of us are needed on this planet, and the outward appearance of someone's life is not always indicative of their inner world or their soul contract. We are all here to learn life lessons from each other. How uninteresting would life be if everyone's soul's purpose and mission were the same?

Affirmation: I am so grateful for my own unique sacred journey and all the lessons I have learned along the way. I am ready and willing to be an instrument of grace for the Divine as I interact with other souls. I consciously choose to honor the light in myself and in others. I understand that life is for learning and that we are all in this together.

_____

_____

_____

_____

_____

_____

_____

_____

_____

_____

_____

_____

_____

_____

_____

_____

_____

_____

_____

_____

_____

_____

_____

_____

_____

_____

_____

_____

_____

_____

_____

_____

_____

_____

_____

_____

_____

_____

_____

_____

_____

_____

_____

Awaken to Your Gift of Dream Power

MESSAGE 5

"It is right for you to embrace what will be shown to you in dream state, so please awaken to your gift of dream power. You have a way of relating to the world that is unique. You see signs and wonders in many stages."

Have you ever had a prophetic dream? A warning? A lucid dream so real that you could physically feel a loved one or pet that has passed over? An idea that turned into a great book or invention? Once you unlock the hidden messages in your dreams, your life will change. Perhaps you are one of the twenty-five percent of people that dream in color. Maybe you see geometric shapes or symbols or communicate with angels or loved ones that have transitioned. Your dreams can teach you ways to solve your problems, deal with relationships, or conquer your fears. The Divine created every one of us with a built-in communication and self-awareness system. Our dreams help us to work through difficult situations or life changes and guide us toward what our higher self truly needs and desires. Dreams help us to get a glimpse of reality and enable us to be brutally honest with ourselves. If you ignore the message, they will keep coming in recurring dreams until you acknowledge or understand the deeper meaning. Sometimes we receive downloads while we are sleeping that remain stored in our subconscious until our souls are ready to receive the information. We often say, "Let's sleep on it," because Divine intelligence often brings guidance and clarity when our egos are resting. Some souls even travel to other realms, dimensions, or galaxies when they are in a sleep state. If you have suspected you have this gift, you likely do!

Affirmation: I am awake and aware of my gift of dream power. I am grateful to have this tool to help me understand my life purpose, to hear my guidance, and to communicate with higher beings. I ask for assistance in my dreams each night and graciously receive guidance for my highest good.

_____

_____

_____

_____

_____

_____

_____

_____

_____

_____

_____

_____

Unlock the

hidden messages

in your dreams.

You Will Bear Much Fruit

MESSAGE 6

"You have sowed the seeds and you are about to receive a bountiful garden. The time will come when you need to choose the right path that will lead you to it. You will bear much fruit as you distinguish that all of your life has been guided to lead you toward light and love."

Sometimes we come to a crossroads where the easy way is not the right way. Life requires that we make difficult choices, and although our angels are always guiding us and hoping that we choose the path imbued with radiant light, they will not interfere with our life lessons, and they always respect our free will. Every choice we make that serves love is like a seed being sown into fertile soil. Often the choices we make cannot benefit everyone involved, but we do our best to choose what will do the least harm. Circumstances and relationships are lovingly set up for us to learn the lessons our soul has chosen to learn this lifetime. We always have the freedom to choose, but sometimes the Universe conspires to point to one obvious choice, and often we are protected from making grave errors. Other times, it feels as though we have been cut off from all communication as we float on a life raft in the middle of the ocean with no land in sight. There will always be tests - this is how we discover just how strong and capable and wise we really are. We learn to trust this way - trust in ourselves and trust in the divine plan that will always come to fruition one way or another, helping us to grow in love, and always leading us toward the light.

Affirmation: I am grateful for all of life's lessons. Some were easy and some were extremely difficult. All were necessary. The seasons of life have taught me the value of sowing and reaping. I am grateful for all the guidance and support I received along the way. I will bear fruit that will last in this garden of life as I do my best to choose the most loving path, always.

Release all Self-doubt

MESSAGE 7

"Release all self-doubt; it does not serve you. Please trust the divine guidance you are receiving and welcome these new insights. Open your heart to love and allow truth to radiate from your being. Come, let us journey together toward your true purpose."

If uncertainty and indecisiveness are left unchecked, you may drift through life, continually sabotaging your next learning experience or adventure. Life has a way of guiding us toward our dreams and will continually bring new opportunities for change even when we feel the most helpless or afraid. Our job is to remain open and aware and act, whether we feel afraid or not. Bravery is moving forward, doing what needs to be done, even when we are paralyzed with fear. Are you afraid of what others will think of you? Of failure? Of change? Whatever it is that you feel afraid of, know this - you are not alone. You are surrounded by your angels, guides, and the entire spiritual team who constantly encourage you and guide you in the direction of your destiny. Even if your earthly family is being unsupportive, your spiritual family believes in you, and they are trying to get your attention and are providing you with helpful assistance. Choose what is choosing you - even if it feels like the odds are stacked against you. Ask for the courage and motivation you need to act, and then trust that you have what it takes to move forward. Be assured that every prayer you utter or radiate from your heart, is heard by Spirit, and the Universe is always conspiring to make your dreams a reality.

Affirmation: I am thankful to have such amazing support as I move in the direction of my dreams. I willingly release all fear and anything else that is keeping me from moving forward now. I welcome new motivation and confidence as I relax and allow Spirit to lead the way.

In what ways am I sabotaging my goals and dreams?

You Have Heard My Voice

MESSAGE 8

"Allow my messages to resonate and take you higher, to a new place of trust. As you welcome my messages and meditations, you will know they are your help. Please understand that you have heard my voice your entire life. Simply come and join me daily. I will happen through you."

It is most beautiful when we awaken to our higher guidance and embrace the opportunity to develop a deeper relationship with the Divine. You may wonder why you have not realized this communication taking place before. Perhaps you were raised to pray and ask but not taught how to listen and receive. Sometimes we must suffer certain losses before we are ready to pursue spirituality on a more personal level. Perhaps old, outdated religious or cultural beliefs have prevented you from fearlessly seeking your own truth and higher guidance. If you were raised by unkind, uncompassionate, or judgmental caregivers, it is harder to trust that your Creator is a benevolent, loving, spiritual parent. Learning to trust and feel safe in the world is part of life, and for some, this is harder to accomplish than others. Whatever your past was, know that it consisted of various lessons for your spiritual, mental, and emotional growth, but the residue from your past does not need to affect the way you relate to the world now. Once a lesson is learned, you are free to let it go and move forward. You have complete freedom to choose a new way of living your best life now.

Affirmation: I choose to trust the benevolence of the Universe to be my help and support. I choose to allow Spirit to happen through me, to make my beautiful contribution to the world. I will continue to nurture this relationship by praying and asking for help daily, and I expect to receive loving guidance for my journey.

_____

_____

_____

_____

_____

_____

_____

_____

_____

_____

_____

_____

_____

_____

Miracles of Love Transform Your Difficulties

MESSAGE 9

"You are sad and feeling challenged in how to love. I alone can love the way love is needed to transform this situation. All I ask of you is to be mindful of the ways in which you struggle to show love. Surrender to me all that is holding you back so that I may redeem a truly toxic connection into a connection of fine silk woven together for the highest good of everyone involved. This way the relationship will be under grace, and miracles of love can transform your difficulties into timeless captions of beautiful life lessons."

All of us have struggled with difficult relationships, and it is not always easy to see the love and light in the soul of every person. The truth is, our soul has chosen certain people to be part of our lives long before we were born because they had a role to play on our sacred journey. People come into our lives for various lengths of time. Some stay with us for a matter of minutes because they came to give us a message. Others, like our family, life partners and best friends, have been chosen to be our ongoing strength and support for the duration of our lives. Ask yourself, "What can be learned from this relationship?" Appreciation of challenging relationships can be gained by remembering that they served a higher purpose in your soul's evolution. No one is perfect, and we all chose to come to planet earth to learn how to love, forgive, show mercy, and practice kindness and compassion. However, remember that it may not be possible to heal certain karmic relationships in one lifetime because everyone has free will, and soul maturity varies in each person. In this case, simply surrender the relationship to the Divine with love, and continue to focus on your own life lessons.

Affirmation: I am grateful for the relationships I have been part of, both past and present. I understand that each one was an opportunity to learn about love. I acknowledge that each of us had a role to play and something to learn from our time together. I choose to let go now and embrace peace.

_____

_____

_____

_____

_____

_____

_____

_____

_____

_____

_____

_____

Divine Timing is Perfect

MESSAGE 10

*"In the midst of storms and trials of every kind, you
are awakening to the truth of Divine love. Divine
timing almost always appears to be less than perfect,
allowing doubt, then proving just how perfect it really
is. Time is a way to keep track of your progress, a
way to measure one time of your life to another, but
sacred space is not linear, not measurable. All that
has happened to date will melt away into the abyss,
joining with all else that has been completed. Once
you have learned the lesson, the structural support
of it falls away, leaving only faded memories, and the
infused knowledge of the lessons learned."*

Spiritual awakening is a lifelong process for every person. All experiences and relationships are meant to help you to learn about the purpose of your life. Each day brings new revelations about your own existence, as well as the consciousness of the entire world. Awakening happens in different ways, and we do not consciously choose when we awaken, for it is by grace alone that this occurs. People often wake up to a new reality during adversity, and that is why suffering is considered a great blessing in many spiritual traditions. Spiritual awakening can be very painful, as it is the annihilation of ego and illusion. Everything may come crashing down all at once, or dismantled slowly - either way, you will eventually rebuild. Questioning everything you were ever taught, and believed to be true, is a fundamental part of the process, and the more you offer resistance, the more unbearable the process will be. As you choose to surrender and enter the depths of the vast ocean of consciousness, your intuition will begin to guide you to the surface where the light beckons. As you allow transformation to occur, you will discover unconditional love, acceptance, liberation, and deep peace. You will view everything differently as you learn to navigate your new reality of oneness with all that is.

Affirmation: I am grateful to be experiencing the gift of awakening. I trust the process of life and surrender to the flow of the genius of Spirit guiding my personal transformation.

_____

_____

_____

_____

_____

_____

_____

_____

_____

_____

_____

_____

I am a soul

having a human

experience.

Your Soul Tribe May Change

MESSAGE 11

"Family of origin is where you learn valuable lessons, and once the lessons have taken hold, people and structure may disappear and then reappear in a new framework to teach new lessons. Changing and growing is always fluid - in motion - never stagnant. People who expand spiritually are constantly moving in and out of various realities. You will soon feel like you've come home to a family who will nurture you into new ways of experiencing life, and this will be so good for your spiritual growth."

If you have recently experienced a betrayal or experienced a loss of friends or family members, take heart. It is virtually impossible to move away from outdated energies and old beliefs that no longer serve you and have everyone move forward with you. Do not be surprised If you wake up one day with a desire to distance yourself from certain people or live like a hermit for a season as you experience inner transformation. Certain souls will remain with you for a lifetime, but there will also be others that will naturally fall away. It is entirely normal to grieve the loss of relationships, but it may be helpful to remember that other souls have their own paths to walk. Not every perceived loss is truly a loss. Are you trying to hang onto someone when you know in your heart that the relationship is weighing you down or wounding your spirit? Have you been grieving the death of a loved one for so long that you have stopped living? Hanging onto relationships that have already reached completion can cause unnecessary, prolonged suffering. Fear can keep you from letting go. Fear that you will be too lonely or lose part of yourself. Fear that you will not survive financially. Fear that the children will suffer. Fear of what others will think of you. Members of your soul tribe will change many times over the course of your life, so be grateful for every relationship, and know that no harm will come to anyone involved by releasing that which is asking to be released.

Affirmation: I am grateful for all my relationships. I recognize that they have all served a purpose in my life. May we all be blessed on our journeys.

_____

_____

_____

_____

_____

_____

_____

_____

_____

Have Gratitude for the Journey

MESSAGE 12

"Always remember, you were where you were meant to be. Have no regrets because you were guided on your journey, always. You made choices, yes, but know that everything happened just as it was meant to. Having regrets is pointless. Remember the lessons and have gratitude for the journey."

If you have moved a lot, changed jobs frequently, had many failed partnerships, or experienced a lot of losses or transitions, then you are likely on a lightworker journey. Constant change and instability are quite often what it takes to prepare a soul for a bigger mission. During this process, you became stronger, more resilient, and more evolved. There will always be people who will judge your decisions, question your motives, and interfere with your plans. Be thankful for them! These are the souls meant to challenge and push against you just enough to find your truth and stand your ground. There were also times that you felt beaten down and had helper souls that came along to help you get back up. Eventually, you recognize the patterns and learn to make better choices to benefit yourself and others. Know this - you have always done the best you could, with what you had, and with what you knew. You may not have always been very skillful or aware as you navigated through the rough waters of life, but you were learning. You have constant guidance and support from your spiritual team of angels and guides, as they are always with you. Certain outcomes are inevitable, based on the contracts you and your loved ones chose before you incarnated. If you are ever bewildered by choices others make, remember that they have their own lessons to learn about their own souls' growth and expansion. Maybe life has not turned out the way you hoped it would, but in the end, all that matters is that you have learned and evolved. One day you may be ready to help others.

Affirmation: I cannot change the past, but I can choose a new way to live life moving forward. I am grateful for the lessons I learned and all the people who were with me on my journey. I forgive myself and others for the mistakes we made, and I release the past with love.

_____

_____

_____

_____

_____

_____

_____

_____

_____

_____

_____

Release what is

asking to

be released.

Know What You Want

MESSAGE 13

"Do you know what you want? Does this elude you? For your life to take shape, you must know what you want. Feelings of uncertainty, along with thoughts that are not focused will simply attract more uncertainty."

To be introspective means to take a good, honest look within yourself. What are your values, priorities, and favorite activities? If you do not know what you want, begin by acknowledging what you do not want. Reflect upon what makes you happy now compared to what made you happy years ago. Everyone evolves over time and it is wonderful to acknowledge all the growth that has taken place. As you objectively assess the new you, you may discover that the old you may seem like a friend from your past. Some of the strengths and talents you have now may have taken your entire life to nurture; other abilities may simply show up. As you consider your job, your partner, and your hobbies, you will become more aware of what brings you joy and enthusiasm and what does not. To know what makes your heart sing is the work of a lifetime. What habits do you have that may be hindering your goals from taking shape? Traveling or moving to a new location may awaken something lying dormant within you. Preferences for who you spend time with, the clothing you wear, the food you eat, the music you listen to, where you like to vacation, and the hobbies you engage in, are all a direct expression of you. Discover what you want and need to feel fulfilled, and then take small action steps daily to create the life you long for. As you focus on what resonates with you, everything that is no longer relevant will fall away effortlessly, creating space for what your heart truly desires.

Affirmation: I am grateful for all the ways I have changed and grown over the years. As I embrace the most authentic version of myself, I know that my light will shine brighter as a positive example for everyone around me.

_____

_____

_____

_____

_____

_____

_____

_____

_____

_____

_____

_____

_____

Patience is the Way of Love

MESSAGE 14

"Trust and believe that things are being readied for divine love to be made manifest through you in due time. There is still healing that must occur for your trust to be fully mine. I am allowing slow progress right now. I am allowing expansion to occur spontaneously, as your soul wills it. I do not control. I use patience, never force, for this is the way of love."

Being cracked open like a seed is the condition offering immense opportunity for spiritual growth and expansion. It might seem like you have been in the damp, dark soil for eternity when suddenly you have the ability, desire, and strength to push up through the soil towards the sunlight. It is there, in the dark, under the surface, that your spark resides, waiting for the perfect moment to ignite. This season is truly the most painful yet enlightening time your soul will ever experience. When you come out of it, you will look back and realize that it was only by the grace of the Divine that you survived! If you are on an accelerated spiritual path this lifetime, you may experience more than one dark night of the soul, and if that is the case, you are truly blessed. Be gentle with yourself as you learn to navigate this new beginning, this new way of understanding yourself and relating to the world and those around you. Eventually, you may be called to share what you have learned and how you have grown by being a helper soul to others. You will be given opportunities to be patient, kind, gentle, compassionate, and wise as you let your light shine forth in the darkness by supporting others.

Affirmation: I honor the darkest, most difficult times of my life, because I know I benefited spiritually from the pain and suffering I experienced. I am glad it was for a season and that brighter times eventually followed. I now embrace my future with hope, happiness, and gratitude.

_____

_____

_____

_____

_____

_____

_____

_____

_____

_____

_____

_____

_____

_____

_____

_____

_____

You are a beautiful, strong, and resilient soul.

See the World Through New Eyes

MESSAGE 15

"You will know when you have broken out of the cage that has held you hostage for too long. You will feel immense freedom, like you are soaring above the earth plane, like you are knowing great secrets, and seeing the world through new eyes."

Imagine in your mind's eye a beautiful bird. Now imagine a rock tied to its' foot. What rocks are preventing you from flying? Pay close attention to the first impressions that pop into your head. Is it a partner? A job? A commitment that is complete? An irrational fear? An old vow? A friend or neighbor who is all take and no give? Your higher self knows what or who is holding you back and wishes for this knowledge to come to your conscious awareness. Ask yourself: "What lessons have I learned? Is it time to let go?" Do not be afraid of the guidance you receive; simply acknowledge the information and contemplate on it. Set an intention to release all that no longer serves your highest good and best intent. You do not need to release everything at once - all in one day - you simply need to be aware that you do have the power to set yourself free from what keeps you tied down. If you sense that something is weighing you down, but you are meant to hang on a little longer, trust that the purpose of the situation may not yet be complete. You will be guided to let go at the right time and in the right way once the lessons have been learned.

Affirmation: I am free to choose what is choosing me. I consciously release all that is no longer needed or helpful for my spiritual journey. I allow the weight that has held me down to fall away, allowing me a greater sense of freedom. As I take small action steps, I trust the higher intelligence of the Universe to sort everything out beautifully.

Relinquish Control and Simply Allow

MESSAGE 16

"When you wish things to happen faster, rather than relax and allow yourself to be guided, it prevents me from guiding you to the best possible outcome. Try to relinquish all control and simply allow my love to guide. It is in the small things that you will see my hand gently guiding. Just trust and surrender to what love wants to manifest."

Intuition is Spirit speaking directly to our personal spirit, or higher self. Sometimes we know far ahead of time what will unfold, and it is hard to resist the urge to move things along faster than need be. It can be difficult to trust the process of life at times because we human beings love instant gratification! The key is to live in the present moment, trust in divine timing, and allow love to lead rather than force outcomes prematurely. Sometimes things move along quite quickly; other times, months turn into years, and years turn into decades while waiting for a prophetic insight, dream, or vision to manifest in the physical reality. It is not so much the result that matters, as the journey and lessons learned along the way. The divine intelligence of Spirit creates a glorious tapestry of our lives, intricately weaving together all our life experiences and divine life lessons. At the end of our lives, we may have the privilege of looking upon this motion picture in which we played the most marvelous role. Like photos in an album, stories in a book, or a map on the wall, all information is stored in our soul records. Nothing is ever lost, as our soul gains eternal value.

Affirmation: I choose to be patient and trust, as I listen to my guidance and only act when I am guided to do so. I know that this this will allow me to have peace.

_____

_____

_____

_____

_____

_____

_____

_____

_____

_____

_____

_____

_____

_____

_____

_____

_____

I surrender all that is holding me back or keeping me stuck.

We Are Never Apart - I Am with You

MESSAGE 17

"Do your daily duties with much love. Show kindness and compassion to those closest to you and remember that I am with you. Talk to me and include me in all things. We are never a part and you have always heard my voice. Be more conscientious of my presence. Treat everything and everyone from the place of knowing that I am right by your side. Let this become your way of being - of interacting in the world. Allow me to be close to you. To happen through you. To speak through you."

We are one with the Divine and one with all. Separation and division are illusions. The Divine understands our human nature and our need to connect and equally enjoys being sensed and intuited by us. The Divine is everywhere and in everyone, found in both the mundane and the extraordinary aspects of life. It is easier for some people to envision what they believe to be God, Source Energy, Spirit, the Divine Feminine, etc. as something outside of themselves. For others, the Divine is deeply experienced within. The more you open your mind and heart to the truth of oneness, the easier it becomes to live a life of love, kindness, compassion, and empathy for other souls. When you begin to view all people as souls having a human experience, you will become more aware of the indwelling of Spirit and the genius of life itself. Whether you choose to believe the Divine is without or within, this practice allows you to become kinder, softer, less judgmental, and more loving. As you live life in this way, you will have a greater sense of responsibility over your words, actions, and reactions and will begin to appreciate your own light, as well as the light in others.

Affirmation: I am one with the Divine and one with all. I choose to include the Divine Feminine in all aspects of my life and my sacred journey. I am held in Her loving embrace.

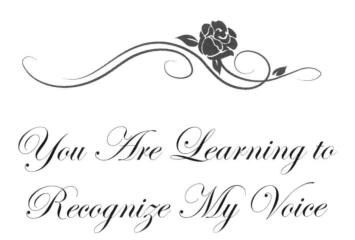

You Are Learning to Recognize My Voice

MESSAGE 18

"You are learning to tune in to recognize my voice and guidance by becoming more fully aware of my presence and my grace. I enjoy being heard. I enjoy connecting in this very profound way with souls that are open to Spirit and love. My grace and truth are yours, as I have prepared you for this since long before you were born. You said 'yes' to being an instrument for bringing love and light to the world. You will show many what changes need to be made for their healing and expansion to occur."

Clairaudience is one of the spiritual gifts that allows you to hear guidance from Spirit (or those in Spirit, such as your angels, guides, and loved ones on the other side) within your own mind. Many clairaudients are already using their gift of psychic hearing without even realizing it. Are you sensitive to sound, and do you enjoy sitting in silence to recharge? Do you gain clarity by talking about things out loud? Do creative ideas flow effortlessly to your mind? Did you have imaginary friends as a child? Are you an auditory learner? Does certain music cause you to feel connected to your soul, and does personal guidance often come to you through songs? Do you hear ringing or high pitch frequencies in your ears? Clairaudience is just one way of receiving intuitive information. There is also clairvoyance, clairsentience, clairalience, clairaugustance, and claircognizance. All the psychic senses are extremely useful for gaining insights for yourself and others. It is always necessary to set the intention that only loving beings that serve Spirit be allowed to communicate with you. Ask for the protection of the archangels, always. Do not be afraid of your psychic senses, as they are as natural and acceptable as your five physical senses. They are Spirit's gift to you, to aid you on your own spiritual journey and to help you to assist others. It is wonderful to discover which of the psychic senses are most dominant for you and your loved ones.

Affirmation: I am grateful for all my senses and unique spiritual abilities which aid me on my journey. I will begin to use them more intentionally to help others to grow and heal, as well.

Ask Questions and Listen for the Answers

MESSAGE 19

"The key is hearing my voice. Be willing to connect with me many times a day. Form a habit by turning to me immediately for answers to your concerns. Ask questions and then listen for the answers. There is no need to torture yourself with back and forth, doubt-filled energy. Ask for the way to be shown to you, and then watch for the signs. Listen and learn to trust that the messages that you receive are from the one who loves you. I will not steer you in the wrong direction. I will protect you from errors. I will defend you. I will be your rock to stand upon or hide behind. You will know when to move forward with courage or retreat into self-protective solitude."

It is comforting to know that when we ask for guidance, we can expect to be heard and assisted. We may receive answers in our own mind through clairaudient hearing, through advice others give us, through certain numbers or signs appearing to us, through a song on the radio, through a scene on a show we are watching, or through dreams and daydreams. When you begin to pay attention to the incoming information and how things resonate with you, you will begin to gain insight into what is meant for you and what is not. Pay close attention to the emotions evoked by any situation and any signs from your physical body. If something excites you and brings joy and optimism, it is likely right for you. If something leaves you feeling deeply disturbed or unsettled, then it is likely not right for you. Does the thought of moving to that certain city fill you with dread? Do you find yourself daydreaming and catching yourself smiling when you think of that certain someone? Watch for doors that open and doors that close. Sometimes, when we are emotionally charged it might be more difficult to hear or see the bigger picture. Meditate to clear your mind and drop into your heart space and then write down all impressions you receive to gain clarity. Finally, trust what you receive, and act when you are guided to do so.

Affirmation: I pray, I listen, I trust. For now, I choose to 'be' rather than 'do' because I know that I am loved and guided and protected in all ways.

_____

_____

_____

_____

_____

_____

_____

_____

Watch for signs and synchronicities.

Your Mind is Powerful

MESSAGE 20

"When life gets too painful, you use fantasy to escape the reality of your agonizing emotions. If you are dissatisfied with life, you try and create excitement. You create imaginary scenarios to mask the pain, sadness, or fear. I will show you in dreams and visions about avoidance tactics, escape mechanisms, and other various distractions you have frequently used to avoid loneliness, unfulfillment, and boredom."

The mind is a powerful tool that can be used to lead you toward your destiny, or it can create all sorts of diversions keeping you in a state of unnecessary drama or limbo if left unchecked. Some people know what they want to achieve, while others will do almost anything to avoid what their soul wants to accomplish. Sabotaging your goals begins in the mind, and the more you think about something and pay attention to it, the more power your thoughts hold. This can be the case when someone chooses to have an affair to avoid dealing with the relationship issues or making themselves physically sick to avoid doing something they do not want to do. Thoughts are energy and can solidify into habitual thought patterns, which can then bring into form all sorts of undesirable circumstances. It is easier to procrastinate or deflect rather than focusing on what needs to be done. The truth is these kinds of tactics can only last for so long. The Universe can be very patient but can also cause a dramatic event in our lives to spur us into action! Fear of failing, fear of what people will think of you, or fear of what you may lose may prevent you from moving forward. If your life feels boring and unfulfilling, it is likely a sign that something new wants to be birthed. Although it can be tempting to watch television all day to zone out, this way of life will eventually become unbearable because your soul seeks fulfillment.

Affirmation: I am becoming more aware of my mind's avoidance tactics. I now choose to move in the direction of my dreams with passion and higher purpose.

_____

_____

_____

_____

_____

_____

_____

_____

_____

_____

_____

_____

_____

_____

Grief Leaves a Lasting Imprint

MESSAGE 21

"Everything in your life has been to ensure that you had family; you co-created your family to create love for yourself. You still fear that people will die. You are often fixated on these thoughts because your inner child was so wounded from the deaths of your family members. Your psyche was locked into a subconscious drive to try and recreate the family and traditions you had as a child."

The life of a Lightworker is often riddled with a tremendous amount of loss and grief. This may even include the physical deaths of those closest to you. If you have experienced this kind of grief and witnessed the transition of their souls, you may have a greater understanding of the infinite reality and the illusion of separation. Your loved ones have not really left; they have simply transitioned into a different reality. Knowing this does not make it any easier but becoming aware of the impermanence can bring a sense of consolation, healing, and acceptance. When someone loses a primary caregiver in their formative years when nurturing was needed most, their soul can become wounded, and the mental and emotional anguish can leave a lasting imprint, which requires healing. Feelings of abandonment, distrust of the Divine, and the birth of fear-based thoughts can then pervade all future life experiences, if not healed appropriately. Blocking out memories, suppressing fears, blaming the deceased, relying on substances to block the pain, or pretending to be stronger than you are can all be side effects of the losses experienced. Life is a cycle of hurting and healing and helping. Self-awareness leads to self-healing. Self-healing leads to awakening. Awakening leads to awareness of oneness. Is it possible that your ability to love so deeply is due to the depth of suffering you have endured so that you could better help others?

Affirmation: I acknowledge all my fears and insecurities and I graciously receive healing for every loss that I have experienced so that I may be an example of hope and healing for others.

Life is a cycle
of hurting
and healing
and helping.

Help Your Loved Ones to Shift Their Consciousness

MESSAGE 22

"I see all the ways that you are learning and growing. I am aware that you are concerned about what you can do to help your loved ones to shift their consciousness. I bless your efforts. You are doing all you are able, and I bless the energetic outcome of you all. I will love them through you, and they will see my light and love and joy and peace radiate from your eyes and your very being. Let your light shine forth."

As you evolve spiritually, it is most beautiful for you to want the same growth to happen for your loved ones. Soul evolution is not something any of us can force or control, as it is by grace alone that this awakening occurs. Everyone's personal soul journey is sacred, and soul growth and expansion is deeply personal. Life is not a competition but rather a series of opportunities designed to teach us all lessons in kindness, patience, and compassion. Your soul growth and expansion have a ripple effect on those around you. The Divine does not require perfection of anyone, but rather a willingness to be as human and as authentic as we can, admitting our truest feelings, getting in touch with our own shortcomings, speaking our truth with love, and setting boundaries with other people. Living in this world is not all butterflies and rainbows, and to pretend that darkness and negativity do not exist, does not do anyone any favors. All that matters is that we try our best to remain nonjudgmental, and to accept others wherever they are on their soul journey. When we make mistakes, we must admit our errors, take responsibility for our words and actions, and always try to see the other person's point of view. We may need to apologize and make restitution if necessary. This is love in action, and love is the essence of who you are.

Affirmation: I am grateful for my own soul growth. I see every situation and relationship in my life as opportunities to both learn and teach, as we all have something to offer one another.

Make the Smallest Effort to Be Open

MESSAGE 23

"Let your words and actions welcome all into your presence. It is confusing for some people who feel drawn to you but are repelled at the same time because you are self-retreating rather than allowing expansion to occur. Make the smallest effort and I will do the rest. You are self-protective because you have been rejected or wounded in the past. As you change your energy to be more welcoming, people will come into your life that will bless you in so many ways. You long for a soul tribe, friends who are like-minded of your new beliefs, and I will lead you to them."

There are many subtleties happening at the soul level based on what is in your energy field. You may be in the process of healing and letting go of the past while still not being fully anchored in the new energy of the present because of your new awakening. Releasing old energy, beliefs, attitudes, and even friendships can all be part of this process. People come and go into our lives for many different reasons, and not everyone will move forward with you. If you experienced any wounding, it is important to forgive and release others, as well as yourself, to move forward with a clean slate. You may feel unsettled and uncertain about many things and may even retreat into solitude for a season. You may simply need time to process all that has taken place, and to get to know the new you, before forming new connections. You may not be able to pinpoint when it happened, but you have experienced transformation! Your tastes and preferences for many things may have changed, and you may now be attracted to different people, colors, foods, creative activities, and music. The new life of spring is just around the corner. When you are ready to come out of hibernation, your new friends and adventures await.

Affirmation: I will be gentle with myself and others as we are all constantly growing and changing. I will honor my need for solitude as well as my need for interaction with others as I experience my own transformation. I look forward to meeting and welcoming new friends to my soul tribe.

_____

_____

_____

_____

_____

_____

_____

_____

_____

Align Your Heart and Mind Energies

MESSAGE 24

"You are learning that when you go against what you really want, there is a disconnect between your mind and heart. This causes your soul to be in a state of unrest. Synchronicity and blessings abound when your mind and heart are united in high vibrational energy which is then used to propel you forward in manifesting your desires. Examine your mind and heart to see where there are disconnects. Imagine the free flowing, fast moving current of electricity. Doubting is low energy that causes light to flicker because it causes disconnects in the flow of the current. This slows down your manifestation abilities. Keep the switch turned on, and keep the light burning brightly with your thoughts, words, and intentions. Be clear on what you want by aligning your mind and heart energy."

Indecisiveness is a negative emotion that keeps you stuck in undesired circumstances. Back and forth, on-again off-again energy is not beneficial for heart and soul alignment. Are you in a relationship that has felt futile for years? Are you in a job that pays the bills but offers little fulfillment? It is impossible to keep yourself positively aligned with your truth if you ignore everything in your life that does not feel right. When you decide to make a change, certain individuals may offer you their opinion because they believe it is their responsibility to do so, and they may even discourage you from taking a risk due to their own fears and insecurities. It may be time to say, "thanks, but no thanks," as you decide to set boundaries and pursue what feels best for you. Your day-dreams and the feelings associated with them can be useful to help you get clear on what it is you truly desire for yourself. Before falling asleep at night, you may want to visualize the changes you want to make and allow yourself to feel the good feelings attached to them. Take small action steps each day in the direction of your dreams and know that your spiritual team is assisting you. Whatever brings you peace, feels joyful, and causes satisfaction is what your soul is seeking.

Affirmation: I am grateful for the opportunity to become more aligned with my soul purpose by healing all disconnects between my mind and heart energies.

Contemplate your
options and allow
love to lead.

You Are Not Cursed –
You Are Blessed!

MESSAGE 25

"You've been questioning why it seems as though others are favored or more blessed. You sometimes feel despised or forgotten, believing that you are less cared for, less loved. Please know that this is not so. You are my child, chosen with a high calling. You must understand that your life on this earth has been full of suffering, but also great joys and favors have been bestowed by my hand. I have watched you suffer. I have watched you cry. I have seen you break through fear. You are much stronger than you realize. Please surrender to me. Please trust me. You have all of the help and support you need."

Lightworkers all have something in common, lives filled with more suffering than most other people. This is not because you are cursed - it is because you are blessed! If you had not gone through the trials, survived the tragedies, or experienced so many losses, you would not be the compassionate soul that you are. You are a wise and loving person who understands human emotions that are experienced by knowing the dichotomies of life: darkness and light, suffering and joy, lack and abundance - all are part of life's ups and downs. There is a time and a season for all experiences, and they have all been divinely orchestrated to help you become the strongest, most resilient soul possible. With the help and support of Spirit and your angels and guides, you will always attain spiritual growth, but the process of learning your soul lessons can be grueling indeed. Take a deep breath and realize that you are one with Spirit, and you could never be denied or forgotten. You are both human and divine and represent the very essence of love itself. The outward appearance of your life does not matter. Everything constantly changes. You are precious. You are loved. You are perfect as you are.

Affirmation: I am perfect, healed, whole and complete as I am. I have tremendous value in the world. I am loved.

Be as One With Water

MESSAGE 26

"Water is emotion. Water is solitude. You are comfortable near water. You sense the magical properties of water more so than anything else. You love rain and snow. You are at home with any form of water. To rest and rejuvenate you need water. To cleanse your mind and heal your body, you need water. It refreshes you as you shower. It is the most powerful form of healing for you. Remember this as you pursue self-discovery. Be as one with water. Immerse yourself in all that it represents. New life. Cleansing. Hydrating. Healing. Think of diamond glints on water and on snow. This is light on water. This is you."

The water signs of the zodiac are Cancer, Scorpio, and Pisces. Water is magical no matter which sign you are, but if you are a water sign then this message will likely resonate with you most. Water is a shapeshifter and can exist as a liquid, solid, or gas, a compound of endless possibilities. It symbolizes purification and represents the subconscious. Water is the universal solvent needed by every living organism, and human bodies are made up of approximately sixty percent water. Rivers represent the never-ending flow of life. The deepest recesses of the oceans in the world are yet to be discovered, which speaks to the mystery of the subconscious. Tidal waves depict the intensity of the rising waters of emotions and feelings experienced by the water signs. Water does not only represent that which is hidden and unknown, it also offers impressions of mirror images on still water. If you are a water sign you relate to the world through the feelings and emotions that you intuit. You are sensitive, empathetic, magnetic, nurturing, intelligent, and loyal. However, to not get tossed around by the current of your own emotions, you will need to seek balance for yourself by welcoming people of other zodiac signs into your life. Fire signs will motivate you in making decisions, air signs will inspire you, and earth signs will ground you, giving you stability and aiding you in making decisions.

Affirmation: I am water, and I flow as water flows. I embrace the cleansing power of water in my life. I will dive beneath the surface to search for the deeper meaning of my life.

_____

_____

_____

_____

_____

_____

_____

_____

_____

_____

_____

You Are Like a Flower Seeking the Sun

MESSAGE 27

"A flower needs sunshine and rain to expand and open and Spirit does this without force, without help. You are all like flowers in a garden seeking the sun for your own good."

To become aware of the Great Spirit, to become aware that we have within us the presence of oneness of all that exists, is a beautiful gift always waiting to be opened and experienced. No one can force this happening as it is a miraculous occurrence that cannot be described sufficiently with words. Once this awareness of Spirit becomes conscious, it cannot be denied, ignored, or forgotten. It can happen in an instant or can be a gentle unfolding over a long period of time. The innate desire to know where we came from and the purpose for our life resides in all of us. As we awaken, we turn our faces to that which likens the sun, basking in Spirit's warmth and light. We are all born with the ability to blossom, as this hidden flower resides within us, waiting to come to full bloom.

The light and love of the Divine Mother is always patient, always kind, always compassionate, always understanding, never forceful or condemning or demanding. The more you welcome this loving presence, the more you come to realize that this warmth and light is the very essence of who you are. The Spirit lives in all of us, as the sun shines on all of us, and does not discriminate.

Affirmation: I turn my face to the sun and welcome its light and warmth. I surrender my heart and mind to the grace of the Divine Mother, and I welcome the nurturing energy and tender care I need to come into full bloom.

"*You are all like flowers in a garden seeking the sun for your own good.*"

You Light Up the Darkness

MESSAGE 28

"You are full of light. You shine and Heaven sees you. The more grateful you are, the brighter you shine. The more you show love, the greater you shine. You are like a firefly at night. You light up the darkness for the world to see. You bring out the light in others. Send love to your loved ones and to everyone and watch their lights become brighter."

Some meanings of "Light," in the *Oxford English Dictionary. 2nd ed., 2002,* [2] are as follows: The natural form of energy that makes things visible, an expression in Someone's eyes, understanding, ignite or be ignited, and having considerable amount of light. We often refer to 'seeing light at the end of a tunnel,' to describe a period of difficulty coming to an end. We also say the phrase 'bring to light' when something needs to be made known. The soul is the spiritual element of a person, believed to be immortal. Reincarnation is the rebirth of a soul into a physical body. The very essence of a soul is a form of light energy itself. There are different wavelengths and speeds of light, measured as the rate in which light energy is delivered to a surface. This determines the intensity or brightness of the light. There are people who have had a near-death experience (NDE), or out-of-body experience (OBE) who have seen other beings of light energy (some brighter than others), while at the same time being made aware of their own light body, which encompasses all of who they are without the physical body. Your light body contains structures of light and is your vehicle to reach higher dimensions and to incarnate or transition back to the Divine Source. Consciously cultivating emotions such as love, gratitude, joy, hope, peace, and faith is like fuel for your light body. You can also send positive vibrations from your own light body to others, as well. In this way, light is increased everywhere on our planet and beyond.

Affirmation: I am light. I am love. I am gratitude. I am joy. I am hope. I am peace. I am faith. I am one with the Divine. I now send light, love, gratitude, joy, hope, peace, and faith out into the world.

_____

_____

_____

_____

_____

_____

_____

_____

_____

_____

_____

_____

_____

Love and Light Is All There Is

MESSAGE 29

"When you send love to your loved ones, they light up. By sending love, you make the world brighter. Love and light are all there is. It is the only truth. Do not condemn or judge anyone; simply send them love. This will bring about great changes. If someone is dull or discouraged, send them love. If someone is depressed or lonely, send them love. If someone is despondent or sad, send them love. If someone is tired or has low energy, send them love. If someone is angry or bitter, send them love. Send love all day long and it will come back to you multiplied. This way, your light will always shine brightly. Love is the fuel for your lamp. Allow love to flow. Be a light to others. Let your light shine. Love and be loved. This is your true purpose."

If you have been raised with organized religion you were likely taught to recite repetitive or lengthy prayers, and to participate in ceremonies in hopes of bringing about change or a favorable outcome. Prayer does not need to be complicated. Every breath you take, every beat of your heart, and every thought you think are offered as prayers energetically. There is tremendous power in saying positive affirmations, spending time in nature, or listening to music that elevates your spirit as you feel the goodness within yourself. You are intimately connected as a beautiful part of the whole, not as a separate being. Nothing you could ever say, do, or not do will divide you from that which you came, which is love itself. As you live from this state of oneness, allowing a greater amount of love to flow, your light will become brighter because you are living from your soul. In this natural state of well-being, you will help others to live more authentically from their souls, as well. By offering kind words and gestures, sending positive thoughts, giving hugs, and sharing your heart and your time with others, your love has the power to heal and move any circumstance.

Affirmation: I choose to give and receive more love and light from my soul to others. We are all one with the Divine, and therefore blessings of joy and peace flow easily to us all through grace and the gift of unity.

_____

_____

_____

_____

_____

_____

_____

_____

_____

Your Soul Chose This Relationship

MESSAGE 30

"You will know when it is time for a new beginning. Your soul is stirring even now, as you long for fulfillment. There are things happening that you cannot see. Things that are aligning and preparing you for what comes next. Do not force; simply allow. _____ has played a crucial role in your spiritual development. Without _____ your soul would not have been able to evolve and become ready for the next phase of your spiritual journey. Speak only good about _____. He/she has been your biggest blessing this lifetime. Although your relationship with _____ has been difficult, it has taught you many virtues, especially _____. You have been a blessing to _____, also. Your souls chose to enter this mutual relationship for a much higher purpose. New and beautiful experiences are on the horizon for each of

you. For now, be patient and trust that all is being accomplished. Divine timing is always perfect."

No one is exempt from difficult relationships, whether it be a spouse, friend, child, parent, or coworker; we all have lessons to be learned from other people. These relationships may last weeks, months, years, or lifetimes. It is helpful to remember that no relationship is one-sided and that both of you have chosen to enter this bond because your souls knew that it was what you both needed to grow and evolve spiritually. Some difficult relationships may be due to a karmic debt that was carried forward from a past life, while others may be relationships you entered before you awakened spiritually, and now you realize that it is in your highest interest to hold onto them. Often when one soul is evolving, and the other is not, it becomes virtually impossible to stay connected. You will know the karmic debt has been paid when you can accept what has transpired and show compassion for the other person while offering them love and gratitude. They may or may not remain with you once the karmic cycle has been completed. Your soul will know when all has been accomplished and it is time to let go to live in peace.

Affirmation: I am grateful for all lessons learned from my relationships, even those that have been most challenging. I have the freedom to choose, with discernment, which relationships are meant to continue, and which have already fulfilled their purpose in my life. I have compassion for myself and others.

_____

_____

_____

_____

_____

_____

Place the situation under grace as you allow love and light to transform it.

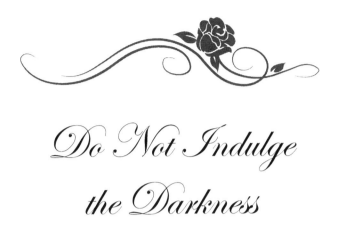

Do Not Indulge
the Darkness

MESSAGE 31

"You have the power to change your circumstances. You possess the light and love needed to transform your world. Do not allow darkness to penetrate your mind space. Shadows are an illusion; transmute them by bringing them into the light. Speak and think and believe only positive. Battles can be avoided by not indulging in the darkness of negativity. Light always wins. Be proactive in your own soul healing and expansion. When a dark memory or judgmental thought comes, send light to them. When a vengeful daydream or night terror comes, send light to them. The subconscious becomes conscious as an opportunity to be healed. Many are the distractions of lower, denser energies in life, but they need not be indulged. Focus on what is true, kind, peaceful, compassionate, loving, and merciful."

Whatever we give our attention to expands energetically. Have you ever become trapped in a state of brooding? Does worrying about work or a family situation keep you up all night? Do regretful conversations play over and over in your mind as you consider what you should have said? Trusting that things always work out may seem easier said than done, but no good can come from guilt, worrying, and overthinking. It takes a tremendous amount of grace to surrender our worries to the divine intelligence of Spirit, but it is possible. The truth is, there are many things we cannot control. What we can always control, however, are our reactions and responses to the challenges that life throws at us. When we shift from a place of blame and self-pity and anger to a place of self-responsibility and kindness, healing becomes possible. First, we need to understand that we are all in this together. There is no 'I' only 'we' in this earth school; we all have something to learn from every situation or relationship. Approach every challenge from a place of compassion and understanding, and allow love to lead, always.

Affirmation: I am learning to take responsibility for my thoughts, interactions, and reactions with others. I recognize that most souls are wounded in some way and that I do not need to take others' words or reactions personally. I will do my best to forgive myself and others.

_____

_____

_____

_____

_____

_____

_____

_____

Be at Peace to Attract Abundance

MESSAGE 32

"I know you have many questions, and it is difficult for you to trust, but you needn't worry or fear because you are a creature of love. Be at peace and know that all is well as this is the surest way to attract heavenly abundance. Graciously accept every blessing, no matter how small, with gratitude and joy. This is pleasing and restful for your soul, as ingratitude and fear cause unrest and block the flow of abundance. Practice allowing your soul to be at peace and in the flow of what is, while keeping your mind clear and free of confusion and judgements. Your heart must be open to love for grace and wisdom to reside within you. Do not allow contempt, fear, or worry into your heart. Ask to be filled with love and light, always. If you judge and blame others, or are rigid and unforgiving, this dims the light of your soul, hardens your heart, clouds your

mind, and prevents blessings and graces from flowing into your reality."

Be at peace. Graciously accept. Be in the flow. Keep your mind clear and heart open. This seems easier said than done, especially when more money is going out than coming in, and everyone seems to want something from you. Your child is sick. You hate your job. Divorce is on the horizon. You cannot manage working full time and continue caring for your aging parents. Your course load is too heavy. There seems to be all sorts of problems, but no solutions. You have been praying for a breakthrough, but instead, more is heaped on. You are in a cycle of blaming others and doubting yourself. The root of blame and guilt is fear. Are you afraid that you are not going to be able to pay your bills this month? Are you afraid that your friends and family will judge you for leaving your toxic partner? Are you afraid your aging parents will decline if you take that new job across the country? You know that you do not have what you need, but you are afraid to take a risk. The opposite of fear is love. What is the solution? Return to love. Turn off the voice in your head that is fearful and condemning and tune in to the voice of your soul. Being tested is part of life, and you will come out stronger and more evolved than before.

Affirmation: I know that no matter what is going on around me, I am divinely supported by the Universal Mother. I will make small choices each day and remain in a state of love so that I may attract abundance in every way.

_____

_____

_____

_____

_____

_____

Do Not Force Endings or Outcomes Prematurely

MESSAGE 33

"Focus on forgiving everyone, including yourself, for all transgressions, as you are all learning and growing together. You are all created equal and no soul is more valued than any other. Every soul's journey is unique and life experiences and lessons are tailored for each soul. Do not judge the journey of any other, simply acknowledge the beauty of each soul's growth and expansion over time. Some of you are connected at a soul level because of contracts or agreements you made of your own choosing. When lessons have been learned or when the purpose of a particular relationship has been fulfilled, endings take place so that new experiences and relationships can begin. This is most beautiful and necessary. There is no need to force endings or outcomes prematurely, even when you are keenly aware of the direction your soul is going.

Cherish and be grateful for all the moments, whether perceived as good or bad, as they make up your soul's experiences."

You may be sensing through your innate intuition that something is about to end or change. Perhaps you sense that one of your children will be moving away sooner than expected, or that your boss will be moving to a different department, or that your partner is disconnecting and preparing to move on. Sometimes you will agree with the upcoming change, and other times you may feel unprepared, betrayed, or angry with what is happening. Although you cannot control what others choose to do, you can control your reaction to their decisions. Every person's soul has a built-in compass that guides them toward their soul's lessons, and therefore it is futile to try and interfere with anyone's path. As you compare your journey to other's chosen paths, can you see the value and uniqueness of them all? There is such an eclectic mix of lifestyles in the world. It is acceptable to grieve the ending of some relationships and celebrate the ending of others. Whether you perceive a relationship as good or bad, try to remember they all served a higher purpose.

Affirmation: I am grateful for all the people that have moved in and out of my life and experiences and for everything I learned along the way.

_____

_____

_____

_____

_____

_____

_____

I forgive myself
and others because
we are learning
and growing
together.

Release the Baggage of Old Beliefs

MESSAGE 34

"Keep releasing old beliefs. You are not tied to any beliefs. You are free to choose your own path. Your path is blessed. You are strong and capable. You are the Watcher on the Wall. This means that you see things long before they happen. You are forewarned in dreams, always. You are shown and guided. Your dreams have always been prophetic. Pay attention to them. You will be shown what to do."

Certain beliefs serve you for a while, and others remain with you over lifetimes. Sometimes when you feel stale or stuck, it is helpful to dissect your beliefs to determine whether they still resonate with you. As a more evolved soul, you are no longer the same person you were five, ten or thirty years ago because you have experienced soul growth and expansion. This is the purpose of living. When we sense change is in the air, our dreams will also give us a glimpse - or a full painting - of what is to come. Will your current beliefs still serve you as you move forward into this new future, or do they feel like old baggage weighing you down? Perhaps you have come to realize that a commitment you previously made to something or someone is no longer relevant, and it is now causing you suffering because it has long since fulfilled its purpose. Your soul will always continue to lead you to true peace, joy, and contentment. Going against the inner truth which resides within your soul may even be creating unnecessary pain or dis-ease in your physical body. When you are contemplating your beliefs, it may be helpful to do a physical body scan to determine whether anything outdated is being stored within your physicality or aura unnecessarily. It is perfectly acceptable to hang onto familiar personal or cultural beliefs or to reach for ideas and spiritual practices that are completely new. The choice is yours!

Affirmation: I am free to explore all my beliefs and to release all that no longer resonate with me. I am unique and acceptable just as I am.

Great Pain Equals Great Love

MESSAGE 35

"If you are to grow in the spiritual gifts, you must be open to knowing even if it is painful. When you progress spiritually, you begin to understand that pain brings growth. You will learn this truth - for yourself and others because it is the way Spirit works in the world for expansion to occur. Pain does not mean torment. Torment is fear. Pain is love. Everything painful holds great value. Great pain equals great love. Think of bearing children. This kind of pain is growth assured."

Knowing is beyond the five senses. Believing is not the same as knowing. Claircognizance is the awareness of knowing beyond the five human senses. This allows you to live life more fully, as you receive insightful awareness of what is happening beneath the surface. If through the gift of claircognizance, you intuited ahead of time that your loved one would be passing over soon, it would feel painful at first and yet offer a beautiful opportunity to exchange words, offer forgiveness, or to simply make the most of the remaining time. Consider the gift of clairvoyance being used for the purpose of helping a family to find a missing loved one that would not otherwise be found. It is the gift of clairaudience that allows you to hear guidance from your angels instructing you to schedule that doctor's appointment that you have been procrastinating about to then find out that you have a medical condition that needs immediate attention. Although it would be disturbing to receive this kind of news, it is a gift to discover the issue early to seek treatment. Clairsentience is the gift of clear feeling. Have you ever been completely overwhelmed by the dark or negative energy of a certain person, place, or object and therefore avoided unnecessary contact? The spiritual gifts help you to effectively guard your energy body, avoid stressful situations, and protect yourself from danger. Multisensory awareness is a beautiful gift from the Divine and developing and using your gifts is nothing to be feared, only cherished.

Affirmation: I will no longer be afraid of my spiritual gifts. I will embrace every opportunity to develop and use them to help myself and others.

Have I outgrown my previous set of beliefs?

Make Choices ~ Be Empowered

MESSAGE 36

"Your freedom comes from your power to make choices. You have tremendous personal power. Embrace this time of your life. This time you will choose more wisely what truly honors you. You have been chosen to accomplish great and mighty things. You will be separated from all that contaminates your energy, your peace. You will be delivered from everything and everyone that slows or stops your progress. This is your time to shine."

Before you incarnated this lifetime your soul, in partnership with Spirit, chose to accomplish something specific and unique for your own souls' journey. The wisdom of your soul knows exactly what you need to experience to achieve soul growth and expansion. As you go through life, there will be times that you feel you are going in the right direction and other times that you sense you have gotten distracted and fallen off track. Perhaps you engaged in a lower vibrational relationship, and now you feel stuck or took a job that does not make your heart sing, but it pays the bills, or you turned down a terrific opportunity because of fear and doubt in yourself. Thank goodness that we are less bound by our circumstances than we think! Eventually, your soul will say, "Enough is enough. There is more to life than this. This is not what I was put on this earth to do!" Your soul will always lead you back to your true purpose with the help of your angels and spiritual team. Then the bumps in the road will seem to smooth out, the sun will seem to shine brighter, and you will feel a certain lightness and joy as you once again become aligned with your destiny. This does not mean that there will not be challenges, but even on the hard days, you will feel much more satisfaction and contentment as you seek fulfillment and liberation for yourself.

Affirmation: I am so grateful that making one small choice each day has the power to align me with my destiny. I will remember to ask for help from my angels and guides each day to accomplish all that I came here to do this lifetime.

_____

_____

_____

_____

_____

_____

_____

_____

_____

_____

_____

Out with the Old and In with the New

MESSAGE 37

"Your night dreams have been telling you that it's time to clean up and reorganize your life. Out with the old and in with the new is the predominant message. Do not fall into fear and worry about the future. A time of completion is at hand. You are being released from that which no longer serves you. This is a blessing. As you make a few changes to assist with the release of old energy, you will find more peace and joy available to you. When you release the past, you will be amazed at what you can accomplish as you embrace this new energy and growth within yourself."

In life, we all go through phases and cycles that are perfectly designed to allow us to become newer and better versions of ourselves. Whatever you are experiencing inside of yourself is always reflected in your outer world as well. If you are balanced energetically and are flowing with life, these natural rhythms allow you the highest potential for growth and expansion. Creation and destruction are equally important in the cycle of life. The old foliage must be shed for new growth to occur. There are many healing modalities that may be used to aid you in this healing, transformative, process such as: acupuncture, crystal healing, Reiki, Qigong, yoga, sound therapy, massage therapy, or aromatherapy, to name a few. It is both unnecessary and undesirable to experience negative symptoms such as lack of abundance, mental stress, excessive fatigue, inability to make decisions, and experiencing various aches and pains, as these are all signs that energy is not flowing freely within you. When there are disturbances in your energy flow, you may feel stuck, lifeless, unmotivated, or depressed and live in constant physical, mental, or emotional angst. When you have free-flowing energy, you will enjoy more peace, abundance, and vitality, and this will be evident in all areas of your life.

Affirmation: I will make time to contemplate, research and take necessary action to get the help I need to release all stuck energy so that I can move forward with greater health, grace and ease.

Rise Above the Opinions of Others

MESSAGE 38

"Do not worry about what other people think. They are on different paths. Their journey is not your journey. As you release these relationships, the connections will be tempered, and all will be healed. Please trust and know that you have a higher calling. You will not be made to fit into any mold. You will rise above the opinions of others. You will meet the tribe that understands and supports you. Those who oppose you will be removed. Allow positive energy to propel you forward. You are blessed with every blessing."

As you seek and find your own truth, your own calling, you may be challenged by other people who may try to discourage you from following your true path. It is best not to take others' reactions personally, as they are likely due to their own beliefs or soul wounds, and therefore have nothing to do with you at all. Your soul wants, what your soul wants, and no one and nothing can stop you from fulfilling your divine life purpose, and it is best to not interfere with anyone else's chosen path, either. We all have a special calling, and it is a great blessing to find like-minded souls who will love and support us in answering the call. The grace of Spirit constantly heals all things past, present, and future, in the perfect time and the perfect way. When certain relationships and connections come to an end, these transitions do not need to be bemoaned, but celebrated because they have taught you well and fulfilled their purpose. Think only good thoughts about the people who have disagreed with or provoked you because these relationships held tremendous value. In time, you will rejoice and be in awe at how everything worked out beautifully for everyone involved. This is the way of Spirit.

Affirmation: I willingly release all people in my life that are not meant to move forward with me. I trust that in time all will be healed and cleared up between us. For now, I choose to honor their paths, as well as my own.

_____

_____

_____

_____

_____

_____

_____

_____

_____

_____

_____

_____

One of the
greatest causes of
suffering is
self-betrayal.

Hold Every Soul in High Esteem

MESSAGE 39

"Forgiveness and acceptance of all that is are signs of spiritual maturity. Hold every soul in high esteem, belittling no one. Practice non-judgement and send love and light to all souls that are part of your life experiences, as all souls require this for expansion to occur. Be the positive helper soul they all need as this is the role of a lightworker. You are well seasoned and have a heart of compassion because you have suffered and learned so much. Do not shy away from this - embrace it. It is your true calling and part of your divine life purpose. Be a true example of love and acceptance allowing these things to emanate from your heart center."

To be a heart of compassion for others, it is important to make sure that you actively nurture your own heart center. Painful life experiences from your past can leave murky, stagnant residue in your energy centers (chakras) that solidify in your physical body if you do not heal and release them. Past arguments, old grudges, betrayals, and other traumatic experiences, along with the beliefs, emotions, memories, and judgmental thoughts attached to them, may still be lingering in your energy body. Nothing good can come from hanging onto old emotional wounds that cause you to feel stressed, exhausted, anxious, or miserable. Only the lessons learned, and the compassion gained from them will benefit yourself and others now. Speaking powerful words of forgiveness, developing a yoga practice, having a sea salt bath, experiencing a sound therapy session, wearing gemstones such as rose quartz or green aventurine, using essential oils for emotional release, or smudging with sage and sweetgrass are a few healing methods that will certainly purify negative energies within your aura and environment. Energy healing modalities such as Angelic Reiki, Healing Touch Therapy, Pranic Healing, Chakra healing, Karmic Regression Therapy, or Shamanic Energy Healing, can greatly benefit, as well. As you experience the benefits of these modalities you may also discover your own healing gifts and talents to share with others.

Affirmation: As I seek my own healing, I will find the perfect balance between loving myself and being a heart of compassion for others.

The Answers You Seek Are Within Not Without

MESSAGE 40

"Just as you wish to know what possibilities there are for you, I wish for you to become aware of them. My mind is your mind. The answers you seek are within yourself. Direct the light on your own mind for clarity of thought. The confusion will dissipate, and the answers will remain. Do not doubt yourself. You may remain as you are, in need of more love, support and resources, or you may awaken fully to your divine potential, so every blessing comes to you without struggling or striving. You may grow cold on your pursuit of happiness, selling yourself short, forsaking your gifts, living in complacency, boredom, and unfulfillment, or you may choose to resolve your fears, embrace your passion, and move forward now. The choice is always yours. Contemplate your options and

allow love to lead you to firm resolve. Awaken now and embrace your beautiful future."

There is no fear of being punished for procrastinating or avoiding that which you came here to do. Time is not linear, and Spirit is patient, loving, and encouraging. Life is about the process of evolving spiritually, no matter how much time seems to pass. If you feel you have missed an opportunity, another will come along. You may find yourself at a crossroad many times on your earthly journey, wondering which way to go next. Suddenly life may seem monotonous, and things do not seem to be flowing like they used to. Then in an instant, you may realize that everything you have experienced has brought you to this moment, even if you cannot see the bigger picture. You have worked hard on your spiritual lessons by seeking, healing, accepting, and forgiving. Although you have experienced many endings, you know that personal growth has taken place through both joy and sorrow. More clarity is available to you now as you choose to consider new possibilities with passion and purpose.

Affirmation: I now know that being stuck is an illusion. There is always enough light to bring into focus the choices that lie before me. If needed, I will practice meditation and be at peace until all options become clear to me.

_____

_____

_____

_____

_____

_____

_____

_____

"Remember the lessons and have gratitude for the journey."

Your Spiritual Success
is Assured

MESSAGE 41

"You are love and light energy. The more you come to know who you are, the more you will be able to transmute lower energies and vibrations to their purest form. You are embracing a life of intuition and love and connection to all that is. Nothing will move you astray from your divine purpose; your spiritual success is assured. You are moving forward, and it is impossible to go backward. Your role is to continually transmit positive, loving energy from your heart center. Keep practicing and continue to allow your heart to expand, radiating love out into the world. Every time you raise a lower vibration, you affect the world positively; you have much to bring the world."

No matter what your calling is this lifetime, your divine purpose is always to bring loving energy into the world. You may be a stay-at-home parent, a lawyer, a teacher, a librarian, a volunteer at a soup kitchen, a nun, or a garbage collector. It is irrelevant what your occupation or hobbies are and whether you get paid to do them. When you get up each day, all that matters is whether you are choosing to make a difference by being kind and compassionate and loving. Nurturing your children, giving encouragement to a coworker, visiting a senior citizen, defending those who cannot defend themselves, buying groceries for someone who just had surgery, or a chemotherapy treatment are all gestures of love. The more you give your love to others, and the more you choose to shine your light in this way, the more you will grow and expand spiritually. The more you become aware of your heart's energy and direct it consciously, the more your love will have a positive impact in the world. If your heart center feels heavy or constricted, it may be time to seek some healing or simply do something loving for yourself. As a lightworker, it is essential and highly beneficial to care for and love yourself so you may better care for and love others because we are all worthy of love.

Affirmation: I am learning when to say 'yes' and when to say 'no' as part of my self-care practice. I understand that sometimes saying 'no' is the most loving decision I can make for myself and others.

_____

_____

_____

_____

_____

_____

_____

_____

Release It in a Sacred Ceremony

MESSAGE 42

"Release what no longer serves you. You are free to choose what comes next. You have a deep desire to purge, so continue cleansing. Your outward reality reflects your inner reality. Rid yourself of all that is used up by releasing it in a sacred ceremony. Write it down. Express it. Burn it up in the flames of transformation. Let it be released to allow room for what is new."

As your spiritual awakening progresses you may begin to realize the importance of releasing outdated beliefs, negative emotions, painful memories, and erroneous perceptions. You may wish to try a ritual to help with this release. Would you like to throw stones into a body of water as you state the intentions of what you want to let go of? Would you like to journal and make lists and then burn them in a campfire, watching the smoke carry all your concerns up into the sky? Would you prefer to sit outside under the light of a full moon gazing up at the stars asking star beings to take everything from you that you no longer need? Would you like to light a candle near a favorite picture or statue or memorabilia, placing all your written intentions into a little prayer box asking the angels to assist you? You may choose to use other things such as prayer beads, sound healing instruments, crystals, or essential oils with your sacred ceremony. As you set the intention to clear out and make space within yourself your spiritual team will assist you so that you may experience healing and transformation. As you engage in this process, your inner reality will change, but so will your outer reality. This is the perfect time to purge unwanted material items and all that weighs you down. Perhaps it is time to get rid of books that hold old beliefs or items that remind you of painful memories. Then you may wish to celebrate your new energy by purchasing new decor or clothing in the colors that reflect the new you!

Affirmation: I willingly release all that no longer brings me joy or serves my higher purpose to make room for all things new, for my highest good and best intent. So be it!

Every person's soul has a built-in compass guiding them toward their destiny.

Be Initiated in the Power of Your Heart

MESSAGE 43

"You have grown immensely, and the time has come for you to rebuild. All your outdated framework has indeed been stripped away. So, what will hold you up now? You are stronger than you realize. You have been preparing for what comes next and you are ready! Be mindful of others, but do not be afraid of what people will think. Your journey is your own, not better, or worse than any other, it is simply unique to you. You are being initiated into the power of your own heart. All things are taking shape under the surface of what you see with your physical eyes. New energy is available to you to propel you forward. Trust that you are entering a time that will be most satisfying and rewarding as you take hold of the new vision."

You are not the same person you were yesterday, a month ago, a year ago, ten years ago. You have grown and changed into the beautiful soul you are now. Life is not static but changing, and everything can change in an instant setting you on a new path. Alternatively, circumstances and situations can shift over a long period of time eventually revealing what has been incubating. Just when you think you have finally settled in your life, something totally unexpected shows up. This occurrence may cause you to rethink who you are, where you are, and what you are doing. This is completely natural in the ebb and flow of life. Do you feel like you are settling? Maybe you were content enough last month, but now you feel miserable. One of the greatest causes of suffering is self-betrayal. Perhaps now is the time to empower yourself by getting in touch with your personal truth. What was it you wanted to be or do when you were a child, long before the world convinced you what was possible or impossible? What opportunity is presenting itself right now? Begin to pay attention to all the signs, changes, and synchronicities going on around you, and soon you will see new possibilities emerging. As you take steps forward new framework to hold you up will magically appear!

Affirmation: I now tune into my heart's wisdom to discover my own truth. I choose to allow myself to narrow my focus on what inspires and delights me.

Live a Life Immersed in Water and Intuition

MESSAGE 44

"When I love through you, you become a divine conduit, a willing vessel to share my light and healing love. You are my clay. Allow me to mold you into a beautiful, embellished pitcher who will both hold and pour healing waters to transform the emotions of those I draw unto you. You have been called to live a life immersed in water and intuition. You will heal souls that require much needed healing at this time by placing all under the grace of Spirit. Simply accept your gifts and act in faith. May your joy be full, and your heart be true."

The tears that you cry are cleansing and detoxifying as they liberate you from the heaviness of the emotions you feel. This form of release helps you to process all of life's experiences so that your heart does not become clogged from suppressing your emotions. The human body is made up of approximately sixty percent water, and the earth is made up of approximately seventy percent water. So much energy on our planet, in our atmosphere, and in our bodies is moved by water. Inspirational ideas often come to us when we are in the shower or contemplating near water. Water is used to baptize the faithful and is believed to bring a fresh infilling of Spirit, as water increases your ability to heal and connect us with your spiritual nature. In Masaru Emoto's book, *The Hidden Messages in Water*, he proposes that water responds to projected human emotions via spoken words or written messages. If angry or vengeful words were spoken the water during his experiments, the water absorbed the negative vibrations and the molecular structure of the water changed. Emoto, used magnified ice crystals to show the differences between fear and hate, or peace and love within the water when it was frozen. Positive emotions caused the ice to form into beautiful, symmetrical snowflake patterns, while negative emotions caused the ice to form into asymmetrical, incomplete patterns. Is it possible that harboring negative thoughts and negative emotions within our energy bodies could also cause these kinds of undesirable changes in the water within our physical bodies, causing imbalances, disruption, or disease? This is good reason to set the intention and make it a priority to release negative emotions regularly.

Affirmation: Repeat three times: "I am healed by water and the Spirit!"

Release all that no longer serves you. Create space for something new.

Take a Stand for the Beauty of Unity

MESSAGE 45

"You are aware of your oneness with all beings. Take a stand for the beauty of unity. Let there be no division of any kind. Teaching oneness is a cry that reverberates from your heart. You exude nonjudgmental, accepting, loving energy for every race, culture, religion, and creed. You love very deeply and open your heart to all. Give and receive love, and do not accept anyone else's fears, negative attitudes, prejudices, or beliefs. Speak and they will listen. Show them the way to their light. They all have it they need only remember. Send light to their memories to dispel the darkness of forgetting who they are."

The vibrational energy of the planet is increasing to a higher frequency of inclusion, love, kindness, and compassion. As lightworkers, we are being called to assist with this transition by not only seeking healing for ourselves but using our spiritual gifts to help others as well. You may be shining your light within your family or workplace as a parent, volunteer, teacher, or coach, or you may have decided to begin a healing practice to offer yourself as a healing conduit to assist even more people with their soul growth and expansion. Love begins at home, but there are no limits to where our love can reach. In fact, there has never there been such an explosion of healing modalities, spiritual self-help books, self-awareness conferences, and consciousness conventions, and people desiring to share their gifts and knowledge through private readings and sessions. This is an exciting time to be alive on this planet!

Affirmation: I am so grateful to be alive on earth. I am awake and aware that the spiritual expansion of the world begins with me. I will shine my light and share my spiritual gifts with others for the greater good of all.

You Are a Spiritual Alchemist

MESSAGE 46

"What is the truth? Truth is remembering who you are as a soul and knowing what you came here to do. A soul must remember so that they may evolve. You are light incarnate. Will you awaken now and come to understand your mission more fully? Keep working at listening, understanding, and communicating with Spirit and your spiritual team of angels and guides. Release all fears and accept yourself for who you are. Do not allow darkness of any kind to penetrate your energy field. Partner with the angels to cut through all dense or dark energy by applying the light and love of Spirit to soul wounds. Heal souls who seek your loving energy but do not take on others' trials, struggles or earthly cares, as all their tribulations are for their own soul expansion. Healing yourself and others in this way keeps the light in the world shining brightly. This

is the mission of all lightworkers. Awaken to your gift as a healer, as an alchemist, by transmuting darkness and negativity to light and positivity for the good of all. Have faith in your abilities. Have love for all who seek your gift of healing light."

Spiritual healing does not need to be complicated. The physical body has the amazing ability to repair itself by regenerating the cells in various wounds as well as growing fingernails and hair automatically. The soul also has the innate ability to repair its wounds and traumas just as intelligently through Spirit. The light resides within us all, but we sometimes need a little help to replace the bulb or repair the wiring by bringing all back into alignment with Spirit. Many different types of healers exist in this world to help us regenerate spiritually, mentally, emotionally, and physically, for our highest good. Not everyone is called to be a healer, but if you are reading this now and experiencing some sort of stirring, then you may be awakening to the awareness that you have a mission as a healing light in this world.

Affirmation: I am thankful for the beauty and simplicity of spiritual healing. I do not need to be perfectly healed to be a light to others. I will practice kindness, compassion, love, and forgiveness as I learn more about the various healing modalities and discover my own unique gifts.

Love is the Knock That Opens Every Door

MESSAGE 47

"Knock on the door of Spirit, and many gifts will be opened to you. Love yourself and others with an open heart and let your light shine. This is the knock. Simple love, like that from the heart of a child is the fastest way to open any closed door. Love will open everything to you. Love is the lamp that guides all you do. Loving with an open heart is the key to everything. Nothing can exist without love. If you are not coming from a place of love, then you are coming from a place of fear. Fear cannot open doors or manifest anything. Fear thoughts are not of Spirit. Elevate your mind, your attitude, your conversations, your beliefs, your relationships to a higher degree of love. Give up torment. Torment comes from fear; peace comes from love."

Loving yourself and others and being grateful for every blessing from Spirit are the keys to experiencing an abundant life on earth. Giving and receiving love is the whole purpose of your soul's essence and is therefore, the fuel that will propel you toward every blessing. Fear is the opposite of love, and sometimes it is necessary to discern where fear may be ruling your consciousness if doors do not seem to be opening very easily for you. Going within and looking at your motivations and negative emotions such as, desperation, manipulation, self-pity, anger, blame, doubt, condemnation, worry, or pride may help you gain insight into your current circumstances. As you acknowledge what needs to change, allowing love to transmute all your negative emotions to their positive opposites, you will begin to perceive things differently and begin to trust that the love of Spirit has the power to open all closed doors. This will allow you to see new possibilities and lead you to new opportunities, ideas, resources, and joyful experiences.

Affirmation: I am grateful to have this opportunity for self-reflection. As I view every situation and relationship through eyes of love and transmute my negative emotions, I fully expect to receive new opportunities and blessings of peace in my life.

_____

_____

_____

_____

_____

_____

_____

_____

Discover what is lying dormant within you.

Have No Regrets

MESSAGE 48

"Things are set long before you experience them. Nothing is anyone's fault; there is no condemnation. Everything was determined and agreed upon before you incarnated on the physical plane. You are divinely guided and uplifted, always. You need not fear any outcome or feel that things could have been done differently. Everything happens as it is meant to as divine guidance is a continuum that does not cease. It flows for all eternity. Free will is a beautiful gift but know that you have been guided in every decision that you made. Divine right order and divine timing are continually activated, and every person's experiences are divinely aligned with their higher purpose. Moment of life and moment of death are predetermined for every soul, and death is a part of life, the eternal journey. These things need not be feared. Love propels each soul forward into each phase of the soul's journey. Have no regrets. Learn what you can and

know that when experiences come to an end, it is because your soul has learned the lesson and evolved."

People come and people go as relationships begin and relationships end. You may find yourself moving to new locations every few years, or you may be wondering why you cannot seem to get away from your hometown. You may change jobs or careers often or get married and divorced more often than you intended. Some people have long life spans while others seem to return to Spirit way too soon. Some people are driven by the need to travel as their curiosity and adventurous spirit guides them all around the globe, while others simply want to sit on the same front porch watching the sunset all the days of their lives. It is so important to live in the moment and to make the most of each day as it comes. Think back to five, ten, twenty or fifty years ago - it seems like another lifetime doesn't it? Think of all the learning experiences you have had and all the people you have loved and lost. Everything in your life happened as it was meant to, and you have always been lovingly held by the Universe.

Affirmation: I know I have always been protected and guided on my journey. I release all regrets, and I am grateful for every relationship, experience, and lesson that I have learned this lifetime.

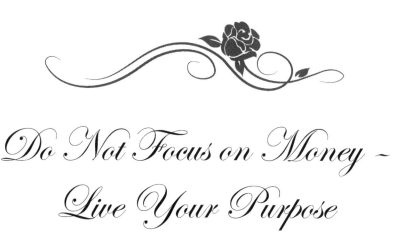

Do Not Focus on Money ~ Live Your Purpose

MESSAGE 49

"You will not be happy or fulfilled until your light is healing those whom you are meant to heal. It is your natural ability to heal others. Believe in your abilities, your gifts. Do not wait for everything to be perfect, just begin. Parallel/past lives are very real and knowing about them helps you to understand who you are and what your soul identity and soul purpose is. It may be your mission to help souls to remember who they are so that they fulfill their soul contracts. You are very loved and protected, and you need not fear the future. Your life will be exactly what you co-create it to be according to your higher purpose, with the help of Spirit and your spiritual team. Do not focus on money, just know that as you live your purpose, you have it."

If you are reading this journal you likely chose this incarnation with the purpose of using your talents and abilities to help the spiritual evolution of the planet. There are unlimited ways in which you can accomplish this. You may be a prayer warrior, a certain type of healer, or you may comfort people by simply listening to, talking with, and sharing hugs with them. Never underestimate the healing power of a hug! You may unexpectedly discover a talent that has been lying dormant within yourself, such as the ability to sing or write, both of which can also be used for healing and uplifting others. You may already be sharing your love, wisdom, and energy as a parent or grandparent, naturopath or psychologist, doctor or nurse practitioner, teacher or artist, yoga, or dance instructor, or as an actor or comedian. You may already be shining your light in the best possible way, or perhaps you have outgrown one way and are about to embrace an entirely new interest. When you are doing what you are meant to do, money will flow into your reality almost effortlessly. If money seems hard to come by these days, it may be time to try something new. Whatever you choose to do, set the intention to serve love and make a difference, and you will!

Affirmation: I understand that self-discovery is a life-long process and that I am lovingly supported by the Universe as I find my passion and purpose.

You Are Not Alone

MESSAGE 50

"Many people believe they accomplish everything on their own. They are unaware of Spirit's goodness and providence. They carry the weight of the world on their shoulders, and their burdens are heavy. Know that their spiritual growth and development will be greatly affected by your love, as you help them become aware of the guidance and support that they receive from their own angels, teachers, and guides. You have grown in love and overcome most of your fears, by learning that you are not alone and learning to tune in to your guidance. Help other souls to do the same."

If you are reading this message, it is unlikely that you believe you are completely alone. You are working on self-awareness and your spiritual growth for soul expansion. Perhaps you are intimately connected with Spirit but have not yet allowed yourself the chance to discover the rest of your spiritual team because of fear or past beliefs. Maybe you know this help exists, but you are unable to connect with the limited use of your five senses, as you have yet to develop your psychic gifts.

Alternatively, your higher senses may be well developed, and therefore you are ready to help others to tune into their guidance and healing for their soul growth. Whether you consider yourself to be a seeker or a healer, all lightworkers are divinely supported, guided, and encouraged, always. The angels are here to assist everyone, and their wisdom and love, and help is constantly available for achieving soul missions. When you ask for their help as an act of your own free will and set the intention to work with them, you will begin receiving signs for yourself and others, and your abilities, gifts and talents will awaken in remarkable ways as you connect with the higher dimensions and realms of consciousness. This is all due to your souls' evolution.

Affirmation: I am so grateful that I am lovingly supported on my soul journey by Spirit and my spiritual team of light. I will try my best to remember this and ask for wisdom and special graces when I am overwhelmed with life.

You are

lovingly held by the

Divine Mother.

Be an Instrument of Healing

MESSAGE 51

"I have watched you grow and become spiritually mature. You are ready to lead others on their journey to light and love, to help them heal in many ways. This will give you purpose, great fulfillment and joy. This will allow me to accomplish great things through your willingness to lead, in love, by example, all of those who have not become fully alive in Spirit. All you need is to do is be willing and receptive. I will happen through you, and you will be amazed with what I can do when you are my instrument. Come, let us journey together and make beautiful music to send vibrations out into the world and beyond. This will attract amazing blessings and opportunities and will ensure your spiritual success and advancement in this life."

To be an instrument of the Divine, capable of helping and healing others, you must first learn your own spiritual lessons and heal your own soul wounds. If you are reading this right now, that means the healing, growth, and expansion you have already experienced is now allowing you to take on a leadership role with regards to healing other souls on the planet. This is an exciting time to be incarnated on earth because there has never been such an exponential rise of healers and various healing modalities. It is a great privilege to serve love by choosing to be an instrument of healing to help mankind evolve. The good news is that we do not accomplish this alone, but rather by surrendering to the intelligence of Spirit, who heals and liberates other souls through us. There are endless ways that this can take place; discover your own unique talents and abilities. In the past, the souls that have been burden bearers are now taking on roles as liberators, transmuting negative energy to freedom energy. This outpouring of freedom energy will propel you forward on your mission as you embrace your calling. You will know when the time is right.

Affirmation: I am now ready and willing to serve the Divine in an even more expansive way. I surrender to love, and I ask for all the special graces I need to live my life purpose helping and healing others.

_____

_____

_____

_____

_____

_____

_____

_____

_____

_____

_____

A Soul Must Be Willing to Heal

MESSAGE 52

"A profound way to heal yourself and others is to send love and light to both thoughts and memories. Everything and everyone can be healed in this way. This is your way of relating to the world; this is where your power lies. Good thoughts and memories are for your joy and pleasure, but not all thoughts and memories are good. When a negative memory becomes conscious, it is meant to be healed for the highest good of everyone involved. As you are remembering, pay particular attention to the feelings and emotions attached to the memory. Call upon the angels to transmute all negative emotions into their positive opposites. For example, fear to love, anger to peace, sadness to joy. In doing this, you will transmute all negative energy that has been affecting you to positive, higher vibrational energy. A soul must be willing to

heal; free will prevents certain healings from taking place. Make a conscious choice to accept your own healing and offer yourself as a healing conduit for others to be healed. Ask, in spirit, the other souls that are involved in the negative thoughts and memories if they are willing to be healed. Trust that all healing takes place according to God's most wise and perfect ways according to each souls' level of readiness and acceptance of healing."

We all know what it is like to be controlled by negative emotions. This is when we are the weakest, lacking in personal power. To remain in a state of love is where your power truly lies. It is our birthright as sons and daughters of the Divine Mother to be able to call upon love and light for healing for ourselves and others. Although we are all here in earth school to learn valuable soul lessons, it is unnecessary to carry forward all the negative experiences, residue, and emotions attached to the soul lessons. We are all here to learn together, to help one another, and to grow and expand as a collective. It takes time and conscious effort, but it is for everyone's highest benefit to release the past with love once the lessons have been learned.

Affirmation: I am grateful for all my thoughts and memories, even those that are painful. I recognize that the emotions attached to them are my soul's indicators of what needs to be healed in my life. I know that I can be free, as I choose to forgive and transmute past experiences as I graciously accept healing and release for myself, and all others involved.

_____

_____

_____

Make a conscious choice to accept your own healing.

You Are a Keeper of Souls

MESSAGE 53

"You are a Keeper of Souls. This means that by your very nature, you take souls under your protection for nurturing and guidance. It is most important that you see only the good in every soul as they trust you and need your light. Do not wound their spirits with harsh or fiery energy. Your role is to refresh and soothe like cool water. Know your role. Harsh, judgmental energy within yourself is only what you have absorbed from other people, places, or experiences. This is not your true essence. Be authentic and careful and conscientious with your energy. The Divine inspires you with goodness to live the higher virtues to be of service to souls."

As you embrace your role as a lightworker, it is important to remember that no one is perfect, and forgiveness of yourself and others is always necessary and beneficial. Have you ever overreacted to someone you care about, hurling angry words or shooting fire from your eyes? You are human and experience negative emotions due to past wounds, triggers, and shortcomings just like everyone else. It is the way you deal with your reactions that matter. Do you genuinely apologize and make restitution if necessary? Healing and clearing your own energy so that you can exude love from your heart and gaze upon someone with love from your eyes is an essential practice for lightworkers. It is helpful to call upon the archangels to assist you with their purest and most potent loving energy. The truth is, lightworkers often attract the most difficult, unhealed souls to practice the higher virtues and healing abilities. Be grateful for such relationships, as they are your best teachers! Having a close connection with Spirit and the nurturing power of the Divine Mother, along with the healing energy of the angels, and the knowledge from your spirit guides will help you have greater self-awareness and self-control over your emotions and reactions. Your spiritual team will help you to clear harsh energies and remain in a state of kindness and compassion. With their help, you will navigate any situation or relationship a million times better than you ever could on your own.

Affirmation: I am in tune with my heart's wisdom, and I choose love. I forgive all perceived wrongs, and I make amends when necessary.

_____

_____

_____

_____

_____

_____

_____

_____

I choose to see only the good in every soul.

You Are Perfect, Whole and Complete as You Are

MESSAGE 54

"Follow your inner wisdom and knowing where mind and heart are united. Work with your gifts not against them. Allow your loved ones and other people the freedom to follow their own heart's wisdom, as this is your role as a Keeper of Souls. Keep learning your lessons and you will grow in your ability to hear higher guidance for yourself and others. Many people fear this process, thereby forfeiting their gifts and talents. Do not be afraid; you are more capable than you realize. As you progress, you will no longer be able to reside in lower, denser energies. This is part of your healing and expansion. As this transition continues trust that you will attract everything you need as you learn to remain in your home frequency by only choosing that which resonates with you. Remember

your innate goodness; you are perfect, whole and complete as you are."

Sometimes revelations occur instantaneously like a flash of lightning from the heavens, causing you to love more deeply and see things more clearly by dispelling the darkness and bringing illumination. Other times, the revelation occurs as a slow unfolding, as you learn to listen, yield, trust, and accept what the Divine wishes to impart. Experiencing negative emotions such as self-doubt, unworthiness or fear may wreak havoc on your ability to tune into your spiritual gifts. Unhealthy habits can keep you numb and unaware of higher guidance that is trying to come through, as well. The good news is that you will never lose your spiritual gifts, although you may need to make some changes and put in extra effort to learn to utilize them. As you awaken more fully, you may choose to just sit with your new abilities or awareness, or you may want to spur into action! As your vibration changes to match your new awareness, things in your physical world will begin to reflect the changes within yourself. As you allow your own inner wisdom and knowledge to blossom, life will seem more congruent than ever.

Affirmation: I am safe and protected in all ways as I awaken to my heart's wisdom. I am grateful for the opportunity to put my talents to good use.

_____

_____

_____

_____

_____

_____

_____

You Are a Red Rose Born of Agony and Ecstasy

MESSAGE 55

"You are blooming, becoming a beautiful, fragrant rose. You have learned to use your thorns to protect yourself so that your buds may open fully. A beautiful red rose, born of agony and ecstasy. Allow your fragrance to emanate to all souls who long to breathe in your very essence. Surrender all to me; I will accomplish all through you. You need not be perfect; all that I require is a willing heart and spirit. I am most in love with your imperfections. I delight in your eagerness to learn your lessons for the benefit of the world's souls."

You endured suffering and persevered through trials which provided you with strength and resilience as well as wisdom and compassion. There were times that you let life happen to you, being bullied by various circumstances and situations because you felt ineffectual and powerless, unaware of your own capability in facing life's challenges. You have learned the dance of life, of giving and receiving, of being and of doing, and you have grown immensely. You now know that it is beneficial to practice self-care and to say no when something does not feel right for you. You have learned that the more you love and accept yourself and others, the more peace and joy you will experience. You are radiating the beauty of your own authenticity because you now realize that everything in your life happened so that you could learn to use love to heal yourself as a catapult to rise out of the depths of your darkest hours. Have you ever noticed that the people who experienced the most suffering and loss are the people most likely to be compassionate toward others? Their unabashed desire to offer themselves as helper souls is the result of the special graces derived from their own spiritual growth. If you are sensing that you have been commissioned for a special spiritual assignment, rejoice! It is your time to shine and to make a difference on this planet. Everything you have been through was worth it, and you are now ready to serve love in a more prominent way.

Affirmation: I am richer because of my spiritual lessons. I am ready to step into my role as a helper soul, for my highest good and for the highest good of others.

The Divine Feminine is the Hidden Flower within each of us waiting to come into full bloom.

Epilogue

I began journaling my personal messages from our Mother in the Spring of 2016. Over the span of three years, it became clear that the messages were not meant for me alone. Over time, I realized that the wisdom and inspiration contained within my personal journals could be used to bring spiritual guidance to not only my family and friends but also all seekers.

As I typed out what was contained in my personal journals so that the messages would be more readable for my family, I began to instinctively add commentaries to what I had previously journaled. I knew intuitively that as I continued digesting and implementing the messages for myself, that they would eventually be shared with a larger audience. The time and attention I spent on this personal project would not only be a way to share practical insights and my spiritual beliefs with my own family but also be a way to bring illuminated guidance to others, as well.

The Divine Mother is always with each of us; some of us simply do not allow ourselves to let Her wisdom come through. Some of us believe Her gentle voice is the voice of angels. Perhaps we were taught that to say we could listen to, and hear the voice of the Divine Mother, would be absolute heresy. All the messages given by the Mother are messages of unconditional love, and therefore they are most beautiful and life-affirming. One of the key themes throughout the journal is that our greatest power comes from our ability to make loving choices. How could choosing to enter a deeper relationship and better communication with our Mother be the wrong choice? We came from love and to love we shall return, but our human journey requires guidance and special graces in the meantime.

"You must choose to love yourself and others, so that your light may shine brightly...awaken to the truth that love is all there is."

You have arrived at the last paragraph, at the end of a marvelous journey of seeking, learning, expressing, growing, and healing. As you read these last few sentences, it is my sincere hope that this journal and the messages it contains has confirmed, strengthened, and established you in your ability to love yourself and others more unconditionally. If you have experienced any form of healing, received insight into your soul's purpose and mission, and gained the confidence to move courageously in the direction of your dreams while experiencing more love, joy, and peace in your life, then the vision has been fulfilled.

"Choose to shine your brightest light by learning the ways of love."

About the Author

Rose is an awakened empath, spiritual healer, channel, and writer. Her soul purpose and mission this lifetime was to incarnate to become a wife and mother to many children allowing her to experience the deepest bonds of family life. Her soul chose the mothering lifestyle to provide her with the relationships and human experiences needed to understand the emotions and archetypes associated with the varied facets of life. The setting of hearth and home provided her the time and opportunity to focus on spiritual exploration as she sought her own healing and the ability to understand her soul contracts this lifetime. Because of her tenacity in pursuing her own spiritual expansion, she has gained valuable insight and wisdom imparted to her from Spirit, the Divine Feminine, her angels, and her guides. Her journey of self-discovery as mother to many, in combination with her relationship with the Universal Mother, has prompted her to write this journal to share the guidance she has received with all seekers.

Life is a collection of painful and joyful experiences that serve the purpose of causing soul growth and expansion. After the deaths of the three earthly mothers who raised her (her mother, grandmother, and aunt), the grief she experienced was the catalyst in her choice to enter a deeper connection with the Divine Mother. This relationship encouraged and aided her in becoming strong enough to bear the difficulties of life. It awakened her to the realization that every struggle, hardship, and loss she had ever suffered was blessed, as trials of every kind were the birthing pains that led to her own soul's evolution.

Rose is devoted to helping people awaken to the voice and healing energy of the Divine Feminine so that they can become better aligned with their soul's chosen purpose. Contained within the pages of this journal is the enlightened counsel and guidance she has received from her relationship with the Divine Mother, along with practical insights derived from her own life experiences and lessons. The messages in this journal provide inspirational guidance, comfort, and special graces to all who read them. It does not matter whether you identify as being masculine or feminine or what your religious or spiritual beliefs are, as the messages are for everyone. Every soul has the innate ability to hear the Mother's voice because we are all Her children and a part of Her great plan of love.

References

[1] Dyer, Wayne W. *Change Your Thoughts-Change Your Life, Living the Wisdom of the Tao*. Hay House, Inc., 2007, p.28.

[2] "Light," def.n.1,4,5, v.2, adj.1. *Oxford English Dictionary, 2nd ed., 2002, p.484.*

[3] Emoto, Masaru. *The Hidden Messages in Water*. Beyond Words Pub. Distributed to the Trade by Group West, 2004.

Manufactured by Amazon.ca
Bolton, ON